God is working all things in your favor. I'm asking Him to equip you with unshakable trust in Him and His timing.

Jesus replied, "You do not realize now what I am doing, but later you will understand."

JOHN 13:7 NIV

There is something God wants more than your talent. God wants your TRUST—(T)otal (R)eliance (U)pon (S)piritual (T)iming.

Marshawn Evans Daniels

DaySpring

God has given you everything you need to enter His master plan and purpose. I'm praying for you to see how God's pristine timing is at work in your life right now.

Now faith is being sure of what we hope for and certain of what we do not see.

HEBREWS 11:1 NIV

Trust is what enables us to access the voice of God with greater intensity and clarity. Building our spiritual trust is the primary way He equips us to experience the incredible.

Marshawn Evans Daniels

God is preparing to **bless you anew.** He is the One who created time. **He is in control.** He's never behind, and I'm thanking Him for positioning you exactly **where He needs you.**

Trust in the LORD with all your heart and lean not on your own understanding; in all your ways submit to Him, and He will make your paths straight.

PROVERBS 3:5–6 NIV

God has a higher, wider, and more eternal view. He knows the ideal timing for you to arrive at your destination.

Marshawn Evans Daniels

DaySpring

You are covered by
<u>God</u>. When His hands
touch your life, failure
is impossible.
I'm praying you see
how <u>His perfect will
and way</u> are so
much sweeter than
perfectionism.

*The LORD will perfect that which concerns me;
Your mercy, O LORD, endures forever; do not
forsake the works of Your hands.*

PSALM 138:8 NKJV

You are a critical part of God's
bigger plan. Know that He will
perfect everything that concerns you.

Marshawn Evans Daniels

DaySpring

God is calling you out of the familiar and into the **spectacular.** I am praying that heaven continues to **lead you, grow you, and equip you with courage** as you learn to live outside the boat.

Let us hold fast the confession of our hope without wavering, for He who promised is faithful.

HEBREWS 10:23 NKJV

Often when we look at our circumstances, our faith is punctured. But it's not our circumstances themselves that cause us to sink—it's our putting our trust in them.

Marshawn Evans Daniels

God is inviting you to rest in His perfect timing, without feeling anxious or the need to be busy. I'm praying that you feel the permission to surrender, let go, and receive what heaven has already granted you.

He who calls you is faithful; he will surely do it.
I THESSALONIANS 5:24 ESV

God is going to make it happen.
Not you. Not me. He.

Marshawn Evans Daniels

DaySpring

The Lord will never let you down! I'm lifting you up in prayer as you dare to trust again.

Jesus Christ is the same yesterday and today and forever.

HEBREWS 13:8 ESV

There is no one more interested in your life than God. His love is perfect and pure, and it passionately pursues you every day, in every way.

Marshawn Evans Daniels

Your future is bright and blessed. I'm praying that your trust in God grows stronger than ever in the midst of uncertainty, and that you embrace the beauty of His mysterious ways.

There is a God in heaven who reveals mysteries.

DANIEL 2:28 NIV

It takes open eyes to see and ready ears to hear a destiny tug, inviting us into the very thing we've been praying for.

Marshawn Evans Daniels

God is madly **in love with you!** You are far from forgotten. I pray you remember that God **hears your prayers** and is interested in every facet of your life.

This is the confidence we have in approaching God: that if we ask anything according to His will, He hears us.
1 JOHN 5:14 NIV

When we pray, we can trust that God is attentive and hears every single word.

Marshawn Evans Daniels

DaySpring

You are a unique
expression of an idea
of God. I'm asking God
to give you a glimpse
of how you fit into His
eternal plan today—and
a peace that passes all
understanding.

*We know that for those who love God
all things work together for good, for those
who are called according to his purpose.*

ROMANS 8:28 ESV

God strategically interweaves our joys
and our frustrations into the lives of others.
He does this for His master purpose: eternity.

Marshawn Evans Daniels

DaySpring

God has made you unique, magnetic, and necessary. Today I've prayed that you would embrace your significance and magnificence in a way that impacts His kingdom!

"For I know the plans I have for you," declares the LORD, "plans to prosper you and not to harm you, plans to give you hope and a future."

JEREMIAH 29:11 NIV

The world needs what you have: your mind, gifts, and personality. You matter. You were specifically handcrafted by heaven for such a time as this.

Marshawn Evans Daniels

You have a special calling. I'm asking God to order your footsteps, amplify your light, and remind you that good works are in your spiritual DNA.

We are Christ's workmanship, created in Christ Jesus to do good works, which God prepared in advance for us to do.

EPHESIANS 2:10

You were born ready to bless others. Start with something—anything— that will simply help people.

Marshawn Evans Daniels

DaySpring

God has crafted you as a carrier of supernatural blessing. I'm asking Him to give you eyes to see the beauty of the gifts He's given you to fulfill your life's mission.

He has given each one of us a special gift through the generosity of Christ.

EPHESIANS 4:7 NLT

Our identity is found in our premade design. It's not about passion—what we choose to do. It's about permission—surrendering to what we were born to do.

Marshawn Evans Daniels

You have what it takes. I'm trusting God to help you realize and remember that you're more than enough to make an impact where you are right now.

Let your good deeds shine out for all to see, so that everyone will praise your heavenly Father.

MATTHEW 5:16 NLT

Your calling and vision are bigger than you. You need God's guidance and grace to see them through. God can't bless actions we never take.

Marshawn Evans Daniels

DaySpring

You are essential to God.
I pray that you would
see yourself the way
the Lord sees you.
May you grasp your
higher calling and
embrace the **courage**
to believe in the
wonderfulness heaven
has for your life!

I pray that the eyes of your heart may be
enlightened in order that you may know the
hope to which He has called you.
EPHESIANS 1:18 NIV

How you see yourself will
determine what you see for yourself.

Marshawn Evans Daniels

DaySpring

God is recruiting you because <u>you are worthy</u> of the incredible. He is also equipping you with the mindset needed to bring <u>Him glory</u>. I'm praying that you would find <u>joy</u> and <u>purpose</u> in the midst of imperfection.

Those He predestined, He also called;
those He called, He also justified;
those He justified, He also glorified.
ROMANS 8:30 NIV

He does not look at your accomplishments;
He looks for your availability.

Marshawn Evans Daniels

Lord, thank You for infusing my friend with Your pristine DNA. Remind her that she has everything she needs to be an effective ambassador and extension of You. Reveal her gifts and lead her to those You want her to serve.

God's gifts and His call are irrevocable.

ROMANS 11:29 NIV

When we look at our lives, we see a mess. When God looks at our lives, He sees a masterpiece.

Marshawn Evans Daniels

<u>Your life is precious to God.</u> I pray you would trade protocol, outdated beliefs, and old conventions for the new adventure God is taking you into. May you <u>trust</u> that God will always lead you well!

The Spirit who lives in you is greater than the spirit who lives in the world.

I JOHN 4:4 NLT

Nothing about God is predictable. The Holy Spirit is uncontainable. His path for you is incredible.

Marshawn Evans Daniels

DaySpring

Victorious is who you are. God made **you** in His image, and He has **equipped** you to conquer every obstacle you face. I pray against fear, and I pray that you would clearly hear from God about your next steps.

Be strong in the Lord and in His mighty power.
Put on the full armor of God.
EPHESIANS 6:10–11 NIV

Curiosity is always the catalyst to calling. The voice of heaven is leading you off the path of predictability and into your promised land.

Marshawn Evans Daniels

God loves to bless you.
I'm asking God to elevate your perspective so that He can show you new places and prepare you for new provision.

Oh, that you would bless me and enlarge my territory!
I CHRONICLES 4:10 NIV

To believe bigger is to ask God for a bigger vision and to believe that you're worthy of more.

Marshawn Evans Daniels

You were made for **greatness.** I'm asking God to help you to trust the **unique way** He's formed and fashioned your personality, thoughts, perspective, voice, and abilities.

Let's just go ahead and be what we were made to be, without enviously or pridefully comparing ourselves with each other, or trying to be something we aren't.

ROMANS 12:6 THE MESSAGE

It's time to stop conforming, shrinking, dimming your light, and running from who and what you were always meant to be, say, create, and do. We're waiting on you...the real you.

Marshawn Evans Daniels

DaySpring

You are God's custom creation. We all struggle with negative beliefs and faulty thoughts about ourselves. I'm praying that today you'll recognize you are who He says you are: capable, wonderful, and chosen.

I can do all this through Him who gives me strength.

PHILIPPIANS 4:13 NIV

God desires that you embrace who you are and grow to operate with supernatural courage using the gifts, personality, and intellect He gave you.

Marshawn Evans Daniels

The Lord is the source of your strength and the force that enables you to grow. I'm asking Him to strengthen you and steer you into all He's envisioned you to be.

When I am weak, then I am strong.
II CORINTHIANS 12:10 NIV

If everyone was perfect, God would have nothing to perfect. We'd never be able to experience His strength. God's muscle is far better than manpower.

Marshwn Evans Daniels

I'm asking God to remove all envy from your life, giving you eyes to see, seize, and savor the wonderfulness He's doing in you.

I praise You because I am fearfully and wonderfully made; Your works are wonderful, I know that full well.

PSALM 139:14 NIV

As hard as it may be to believe, what God is doing in the lives of others has absolutely nothing to do with what He is seeking to do in you!

Marshawn Evans Daniels

DaySpring

Your voice matters.
I'm thanking God for
you today: for the way
He made you in His
image and gifted you
with the **unique power**
to speak life.

By the word of the Lord the
heavens were made, and all the
host of them by the breath of His mouth.

PSALM 33:6 NKJV

God uses His voice to create new ideas,
miracles, and solutions. Embracing
His voice is the vision and the vehicle
to your promised land.

Marshawn Evans Daniels

The Lord is strengthening you. He wastes nothing. Even in the midst of obstacles, I'm thanking Him for equipping you with greater wisdom, vulnerability, and patience.

Now I want you to know, brothers and sisters, that what has happened to me has actually served to advance the gospel.

PHILIPPIANS 1:12 NIV

Your struggles are connected to your calling. Others will learn to overcome, conquer, and find their path forward by hearing the word of your testimony.

Marshawn Evans Daniels

God has made you **distinctive by design!** I'm asking Him to remove any stubbornness or superficial attachments that would block you from leading in alignment with your assignment.

We are God's masterpiece. He has created us anew in Christ Jesus, so we can do the good things He planned for us long ago.

EPHESIANS 2:10 NLT

Becoming who God made you isn't about discovering who you are; it's about becoming more aware of how God naturally designed you to shine.

Marshawn Evans Daniels

I see leadership
in you, planted
intentionally by God.
I'm asking Him to
reveal your assignment
and equip you to
serve passionately
and proficiently.

*I chose you and appointed you that
you should go and bear fruit, and that
your fruit should remain, that whatever you
ask the Father in My name He may give you.*

JOHN 15:16 NKJV

**True leadership unfolds when you
embrace how God has uniquely
wired you to make His name known.**

Marshawn Evans Daniels

DaySpring

You are a **supernatural weapon** fully equipped to **defeat the enemy.** I'm praying God will continue to cover you as you extend His **love, grace, forgiveness, and creativity.**

The weapons we fight with are not the weapons of the world. On the contrary, they have divine power to demolish strongholds.

II CORINTHIANS 10:4 NIV

Everything about you—your mind and personality is an intentional strategy designed to advance the Kingdom.

Marshawn Evans Daniels

Today I'm thanking God for the way He designed you. I'm asking Him to fill you with focus, discipline, curiosity, and mastery as you fulfill His mission.

The one whom God has sent speaks the words of God, for God gives the Spirit without limit.

JOHN 3:34 NIV

You're a masterpiece, an essential component in God's master plan.

Marshawn Evans Daniels

I'm asking the Lord
to give you the courage
to embrace change.
I declare that all
things are working for
your good and His glory.
May His purpose prevail.

Many are the plans in a person's heart,
but it is the LORD's purpose that prevails.
PROVERBS 19:21 NIV

**Disruption in our lives is designed
to reposition us, elevate us, and
propel us into stronger, wiser, and
more anointed versions of ourselves.**

Marshawn Evans Daniels

None of us are entitled to have things go our way, but nothing is ultimately sweeter than God's way! Today I'm asking God to help you wear situations loosely as you trust Him.

They did not thirst when He led them through the deserts; He made water flow for them from the rock; He split the rock and water gushed out.

ISAIAH 48:21 NIV

Following Christ does not exempt you from hardship. The good news is that you're never alone. You're being developed for greater deployment.

Marshawn Evans Daniels

You are not forgotten.
I'm standing with you
in prayer, watching
Him guide you deeper
into His peace and
power-filled presence.

Be strong and courageous.
Do not be afraid; do not be
discouraged, for the LORD your
God will be with you wherever you go.
JOSHUA 1:9 NIV

God doesn't abandon us
the way imperfect people
and unpredictable circumstances do.

Marshawn Evans Daniels

Difficulty doesn't disqualify us from destiny. I'm praying that any disruptions in your life will become paths for greater intimacy, impact, and influence with God.

Do not be afraid, for I have ransomed you.
I have called you by name; you are Mine.

ISAIAH 43:1 NLT

Fixed beliefs about ourselves block us from God's master purpose. For this reason, God disrupts our formed identity to redirect us into our born identity.

Marshawn Evans Daniels

DaySpring

A higher dimension is calling you. I'm thanking God for holding your hand as He takes you to new heights!

From the ends of the earth I call to you,
I call as my heart grows faint; lead me to
the rock that is higher than I.

PSALM 61:2 NIV

God's plans are a firm yet elevated foundation upon which we can build a life grounded in higher purpose.

Marshawn Evans Daniels

I'm praying that instead of fear and <u>frustration</u>, you will have the <u>mindset</u> and <u>heart</u> you need to navigate <u>transition</u> with <u>peace</u> and <u>forward-focused faith.</u>

I will instruct you and teach you in the way you should go; I will counsel you and watch over you.

PSALM 32:8

Seek God's heart. Ask for patience, perspective, and endurance; and may you believe bigger than the obstacle in front of you.

Marshawn Evans Daniels

DaySpring

I'm praying you'll believe beyond where you've been and how things seem. God built you for the journey ahead!

"For I know the plans I have for you," declares the LORD, "plans to prosper you and not to harm you, plans to give you hope and a future."

JEREMIAH 29:11 NIV

Faith steps are your best next steps.

Marshawn Evans Daniels

DaySpring

I'm asking God to help you see the bigger picture when the present moment is challenging your trust. Lay down your plans, and His process and purpose will take flight.

These trials will show that your faith is genuine. It is being tested as fire tests and purifies gold—though your faith is far more precious than mere gold.

I PETER 1:7 NLT

Surrendering to God's will aligns us with our divine assignment.

Marshawn Evans Daniels

May the Spirit of the Lord guide you, guard you, and grow the real spiritual giant within you.

Stop judging by mere appearances,
but instead judge correctly.

JOHN 7:24 NIV

God has already overcome every
obstacle we could ever face.
Don't let appearances stop you
from seeing the unseen, mighty
hand of God at work in your life.

Marshawn Evans Daniels

DaySpring

It's time to let go of
what no longer belongs.
I'm praying that God
will make you a graceful,
courageous, and joyous
navigator of change.
May your blessings
and burdens all bring
Him glory.

*Forget the former things; do not dwell on the
past. See, I am doing a new thing!*

ISAIAH 43:18–19 NIV

Hold fast to a higher vision,
and believe in the greater mission
that God is preparing you for right now.

Marshawn Evans Daniels

I'm praying that you will let go of all fear, disbelief, hesitation, worry, and doubt so that you can shift into the future with crazy faith, trusting Him no matter what.

All things, whatsoever ye shall ask in prayer, believing, ye shall receive.
MATTHEW 21:22 KJV

Prayer is the pathway to God's heart, and belief is what enables our petition to pass through.

Marshawn Evans Daniels

You are limitless!
God has equipped
you with His DNA
and <u>unlimited abilities.</u>
I'm asking Him to
help you <u>trust</u> and
<u>embrace</u> His great
power at work in you.

"Not by might nor by power,
but by My Spirit," says the LORD Almighty.
ZECHARIAH 4:6 NIV

Miracles happen when we take our hands
off and allow the Holy Spirit to be
fully hands-on. It's all easy for God.

Marshawn Evans Daniels

DaySpring

God is a secure place to invest your trust and your heart's desires. I'm praying that He aligns your thoughts, will, purpose, and plans with His.

I make known the end from the beginning, from ancient times, what is still to come. I say, "My purpose will stand, and I will do all that I please.

ISAIAH 46:10 NIV

In order for us to believe the promises of God, we have to first trust the character, nature, and unchanging essence of God.

Marshawn Evans Daniels

I'm thanking God for bringing you through the hard times, and for <u>preparing your heart, mind, and spirit</u> for the amazing future <u>He has for you.</u>

I press toward the mark for the prize of the high calling of God in Christ Jesus.

PHILIPPIANS 3:14 KJV

We are to learn from the past, but we cannot live there. God's mercies, gifts, and blessings are new each and every day.

Marshawn Evans Daniels

DaySpring

There is no limit to what God can and will do. I'm praying that you'll experience His **guidance, goodness, and grace** today.

Let us seize and hold tightly the confession of our hope without wavering, for He who promised is reliable and trustworthy and faithful [to His word].
HEBREWS 10:23 AMP

God has an infinite number of ways—far beyond our comprehension—to bless, guide, heal, and fulfill His every promise and plan.

Marshawn Evans Daniels

DaySpring

God is inviting you to believe <u>bigger</u>. I'm praying that you'd separate from any thought that doesn't line up with God's Word so you can be <u>fully</u> <u>equipped</u> to experience the <u>incredible</u>.

Fix your thoughts on what is true, and honorable, and right, and pure, and lovely, and admirable. Think about things that are excellent and worthy of praise.

PHILIPPIANS 4:8 NLT

Our thoughts make way for our feelings, and our feelings influence our choices, perceptions, and, ultimately, our beliefs.

Marshawn Evans Daniels

God is doing a **great work in you, around you,** and **for you!** I'm praying for **excellence, abundance,** and **wellness** to be yours now and forever.

The tongue has the power of life and death,
and those who love it will eat its fruit.
PROVERBS 18:21 NIV

Declare your desire. Speak what you
seek until you see what you've said.

Marshawn Evans Daniels

DaySpring

You are a magnet for miracles and a vessel for God's glory. I'm asking Him to amaze you with all He can do for you and through you!

I am the LORD, the God of all mankind. Is anything too hard for Me?

JEREMIAH 32:27 NIV

God is always leading you to a blessing or a breakthrough.

Marshawn Evans Daniels

You're on the **right path.** Today I've asked the Lord to guide you through difficulty and into the **majestic destiny** that is already waiting for you.

As for you, be strong and do not give up,
for your work will be rewarded.

II CHRONICLES 15:7 NIV

God uses obstacles to strengthen
us the way weights build muscle.

Marshawn Evans Daniels

DaySpring

God has prebuilt you as a carrier of supernatural goodness. I'm praying that His Spirit would flow from within you exponentially.

Whoever believes in Me, as Scripture has said, rivers of living water will flow from within them.

JOHN 7:38 NIV

Jesus uses a river to explain one of the greatest gifts of being a carrier of the Spirit of Jesus Christ. He specifically decreed that multiple streams of living water will flow from within us when we believe.

Marshawn Evans Daniels

The Father cares about your **heart** and **mind** so much. I'm asking Him to help you take negative thoughts captive, and to replace them with **fearless focus and faith.**

The wise woman builds her house, but with her own hands the foolish one tears hers down.
PROVERBS 14:1 NIV

Doubting yourself is really doubting God.

Marshawn Evans Daniels

DaySpring

You are beyond worthy
of wonderful support.
The Lord did not design
you to operate with
fear in any area of your
life. I'm asking Him
to surround you with
a sound circle of love,
wisdom, and boldness.

As iron sharpens iron,
so one person sharpens another.
PROVERBS 27:17 NIV

Our lives are intentionally interconnected.
The very wisdom you need to make your
shift will likely come from a messenger
you're least likely to expect.

Marshawn Evans Daniels

It's time to embrace your lane, gifts, and assignment. As He expands your territory, I'm praying that you'll keep your eyes focused on Him and the one-of-a-kind plans He has for you.

Let's just go ahead and be what we were made to be, without enviously or pridefully comparing ourselves with each other, or trying to be something we aren't.

ROMANS 12:6 THE MESSAGE

Comparison cripples our confidence and compromises our calling.

Marshawn Evans Daniels

DaySpring

You're ready for this season.

Today I've asked God to give you a trusting heart as He guides you in the way you should go with boldness, decisiveness, expectancy, and surrender.

If you wait for perfect conditions, you will never get anything done.
ECCLESIASTES 11:4 TLB

God rarely performs miracles in perfect conditions.

Marshawn Evans Daniels

God designed you
as a way maker.
I pray God gives
you the wisdom to
discern what to pay
attention to and what
to ignore as you press
deeper into your destiny.

*Here is a boy with five small
barley loaves and two small fish,
but how far will they go among so many?*

JOHN 6:9 NIV

**A key secret to a major life shift
is speaking faith and not facts.**

Marshawn Evans Daniels

God prunes our lives because our purpose is too important for weeds to limit our growth. I'm praying that you would release, without hesitation, all that no longer belongs in your life, head, heart, or hands.

A time to search and a time to quit searching.
A time to keep and a time to throw away.

ECCLESIASTES 3:6 NLT

Clinging to what God needs you to release blocks the very space He needs available to bless you and build you in a bigger, better way.

Marshawn Evans Daniels

God is reorganizing your life to make room for **greater glory.** I'm asking God to provide you with the **insight and courage** necessary to delete anything that takes you off the course of **your calling.**

Look straight ahead, and fix your eyes on what lies before you.
PROVERBS 4:25 NLT

Everything that glitters isn't God.

Marshawn Evans Daniels

Today I'm asking the Lord to free you from the quicksand of people pleasing. May His validation be all you need.

Am I now trying to win the approval of human beings, or of God? Or am I trying to please people? If I were still trying to please people, I would not be a servant of Christ.

GALATIANS 1:10 NIV

God intricately and irrevocably stamped you with His majesty and matchless mark of approval!

Marshawn Evans Daniels

As you learn to accept what can't be explained, I'm asking God to give you a vision bigger than blame. May you speak life into what you seek, not what you've seen.

Be kind to one another, compassionate, forgiving each other, just as God in Christ also has forgiven you.
EPHESIANS 4:32 NASB

Embrace the blessings of betrayal. God uses hardship to propel us into leadership.

Marshawn Evans Daniels

DaySpring

There is nothing holy about hiding. <u>You are magnificent.</u> You have incredible gifts. And you are here to be <u>a light that leads others to Christ.</u>

And God said, "Let there be light,"
and there was light.

GENESIS 1:3 NIV

When God said "Let there be light,"
He was giving you permission to shine.

Marshawn Evans Daniels

God has a new dimension of power, purpose, and prosperousness for you. It can only be found in entering divine stillness. I'm praying that you settle into His goodness and grace today.

Be still, and know that I am God;
I will be exalted among the nations,
I will be exalted in the earth.

PSALM 46:10 NIV

Stillness is a success strategy—
one that prepares us to receive the
majestic and to be an usherer of miracles.

Marshawn Evans Daniels

I prayed today that God would give you a heart aligned with His vision, direction, and protection. As His daughter, you have nothing to worry about.

Surrender your anxiety. Be still and realize that I am God. I am God above all the nations, and I am exalted throughout the whole earth.

PSALM 46:10 TPT

God longs to spend time with you—
to remind you that He loves you,
leads you, and needs you.

Marshawn Evans Daniels

DaySpring

Where you feel impatience, I'm praying you see God's bigger plan to turn it into **endurance.** May He give you **eyes to see** and the **faith to believe** that your miracle is already in progress.

The Lord God is a sun and shield;
the Lord bestows favor and honor;
no good thing does He withhold from
those whose walk is blameless.
PSALM 84:11 NIV

You matter too much for God to give you an unfinished blessing.

Marshawn Evans Daniels

DaySpring

May God quiet the
noise that distracts
you from the voice
of destiny.
May He attune
your ear to Him alone.

*The one who sent Me is with Me; He has not left
Me alone, for I always do what pleases Him.*

JOHN 8:29 NIV

We can't merely desire to please God.
To hear Him, we must also actively
pursue Him.

Marshawn Evans Daniels

DaySpring

I pray that God would turn doubt into **extreme reliance** on the Him. **He is worthy of your trust** in His impeccable timing—He **always comes through.**

Be anxious for nothing, but in everything by prayer and supplication, with thanksgiving, let your requests be made known to God.

PHILIPPIANS 4:6 NKJV

Only God can guide you into your Promised Land.

Marshawn Evans Daniels

Nothing is <u>sweeter</u> or <u>stronger</u> than God's presence. May you dare to <u>believe</u> that His presence and the <u>purpose, gifts, and voice</u> He has given you are <u>more than enough.</u>

My soul finds rest in God alone;
my salvation comes from Him.
PSALM 62:1 NIV

When our hearts are aligned with God's,
He can lead us into the incredible.

Marshawn Evans Daniels

DaySpring

God is inviting you to **REST** in Him as a **lifestyle—not just a vacation.** Today my prayer is that you'll discover an excursion in Him that you never want to return from.

*Keep company with Me and you'll
learn to live freely and lightly.*
MATTHEW 11:30 THE MESSAGE

**True REST happens when we
(R)elease (E)very (S)abotaging (T)hought.**

Marshawn Evans Daniels

DaySpring

Today I'm asking God to clear the clutter from every area of your life. <u>May He make your mind a sanctuary for His presence.</u>

Peace I leave with you; My peace I give you.
I do not give to you as the world gives. Do not let
your hearts be troubled and do not be afraid.

JOHN 14:27 NIV

You are a house of miracles.

Marshawn Evans Daniels

DaySpring

As I pray for you
and your destiny,
I am confident that
God is seeking to
unveil fresh revelation
for your life. May He
fan into flame your
passion for His presence
like never before.

All those the Father gives Me
will come to Me, and whoever
comes to Me I will never drive away.

JOHN 6:37 NIV

When God calls us to deeper and
higher levels of communion,
He does not use condemnation.
He uses invitation and affirmation.

Marshawn Evans Daniels

DaySpring

When I pray for you,
I pray with anticipation.
Because I know that
God is building you
from the inside out,
making you the blessing
He built you to be.

*But seek ye first the kingdom of God,
and His righteousness; and all these
things shall be added unto you.*

MATTHEW 6:33 KJV

Creating time and space for solitude
and communion with God is how
God shapes us and supplies us
for the "more" He has in store for us.

Marshawn Evans Daniels

Today I'm asking God to bless your mind. May He amplify your courage, open your spiritual eyes, and help you embrace, without fear, the incredible potential inside you.

Blessed is she who has believed that the Lord would fulfill His promises to her!

LUKE 1:45 NIV

Belief precedes the blessing. In fact, it invites it. Better yet, it unleashes it.

Marshawn Evans Daniels

DaySpring

God's love for you is a <u>safe place to find rest and redirection.</u> I'm praying you'd move boldly into God's vision and leading without delay. Your <u>destiny</u> and <u>His glory</u> await.

*Does the L<small>ORD</small> delight in burnt offerings
and sacrifices as much as in obeying the L<small>ORD</small>?
To obey is better than sacrifice, and to heed
is better than the fat of rams.*

I SAMUEL 15:22 NIV

Obedience isn't a heavy thing; it's a holy thing.

Marshawn Evans Daniels

DaySpring

God is more concerned with our character than our calling. I pray that you would find a new level of tenderness and intimacy with the Lord so that He can fashion your heart in His image.

The sacrifice you desire is a broken spirit. You will not reject a broken and repentant heart, O God.

PSALM 51:17 NLT

Obedience isn't supposed to be this ominous, heavy thing. It's an invitation to enter a faith adventure with God.

Marshawn Evans Daniels

DaySpring

God wants to take
you into the territory
He has already prepared
for you. I'm praying
that His direction for
you becomes <u>clear</u>—
<u>and exciting!</u>—as you
lay down your agenda
for His plans.

*The LORD your God will bless you in
the land He is giving you.*
DEUTERONOMY 28:8 NLT

God won't bless you where
you no longer belong.

Marshawn Evans Daniels

DaySpring

God is using your
life to showcase the
power of belief in Him.
May you joyously follow
His lead and let Him
architect something
spectacular—
a masterpiece only
heaven can build.

By faith Noah, being warned of God of things
not seen as yet . . . prepared an ark to the
saving of his house . . . and became heir of the
righteousness which is by faith.
HEBREWS 11:7 KJV

Obedience is the passageway
into supernatural overflow.

Marshawn Evans Daniels

The Lord makes a
way out of no way.
He's already planned
a _pathway_ through the
valley of impossibility.
May you move forward
with _faith and focus_
into the _fantastic future_
He has for you.

**Unfavorable life circumstances
often invite God's unbeatable favor.**

Marshawn Evans Daniels

No circumstance is too difficult for the Lord to **achieve victory.** May you remember that God made you a divinely dangerous woman fully equipped to **slay fear, defeat the enemy,** and lead others **into eternity.**

When you walk, your steps will not be hampered; when you run, you will not stumble.
PROVERBS 4:12 NIV

The danger isn't where you are going; the danger is where you're staying.

Marshawn Evans Daniels

DaySpring

God has paved a great lane for you to travel! I'm asking Him to drench you in <u>His presence</u> as you walk unapologetically in <u>His gifts</u> and assignment.

Now the Lord is that Spirit: and where the Spirit of the Lord is, there is liberty.
II CORINTHIANS 3:17 KJV

Going where God guides is less about working harder and more about trusting deeper.

Marshawn Evans Daniels

I'm asking God to remove anything that is standing in the way of you accomplishing your God-given purpose and experiencing His joy and peace in your life.

The LORD said to me, "Do not say, 'I am too young.' You must go to everyone I send you to and say whatever I command you. Do not be afraid of them, for I am with you and will rescue you," declares the LORD.

JEREMIAH 1:7–8 NIV

Beautiful is a woman in alignment with her divine assignment.

Marshawn Evans Daniels

God has <u>destined you to lead!</u> My prayer for you is for upgraded thinking. May you step into the big shift happening around you, for you, and through you.

The LORD had said to Abram,
"Go from your country, your people and your father's
household to the land I will show you."

GENESIS 12:1 NIV

When you go wherever God sends you,
people get a greater glimpse of Him,
which is what He's after.

Marshawn Evans Daniels

You are at the
forefront of God's
mind. Everything that
concerns you matters to
God! Every detail.
I'm praying that you live
boldly, knowing your
future is secure.

I have engraved you on the palms of My hands;
your walls are ever before Me.
ISAIAH 49:16 NIV

We are etched into the very fiber of
who God is. We can never be off His radar.

Marshawn Evans Daniels

You are necessary because God said so. May you root yourself in this truth to such an extent that you experience His beauty and sweetness like never before.

You are a chosen race, a royal priesthood, a holy nation, a people for His own possession, that you may proclaim the excellencies of Him who called you out of darkness into His marvelous light.

I PETER 2:9 ESV

What God has taken you through is all about what God is taking you to.

Marshawn Evans Daniels

You are a warrior
filled with God's
mighty power, love,
and incredible mind.
I asked God to remind
you of this today.

God will never give you the spirit of fear,
but the Holy Spirit who gives you mighty
power, love, and self-control.
II TIMOTHY 1:7 TPT

When fear knocks, allow faith to answer.

Marshawn Evans Daniels

You are a magnificent light. May you embrace it and never dim the radiance of God DNA that shines from within you. I pray heaven releases your brilliance like never before.

You are altogether beautiful, my darling; there is no flaw in you.

SONG OF SONGS 4:7 NIV

Beautifulness is what we crave—not because we need it, lost it, or must attain it as the world says but because it is who we already are.

Marshawn Evans Daniels

DaySpring

God is using your life, your story, and your struggles to expand the world's perception of Him. My prayer is for you to grow as His ambassador in circles large and small.

Don't hide your light! Let it shine for all;
let your good deeds glow for all to see,
so that they will praise your heavenly Father.

MATTHEW 5:15–16 TLB

Your story is a sign of God's strength.

Marshawn Evans Daniels

DaySpring

God has already called you worthy and wonderful. I'm asking Him to surround you with extraordinary wisdom so that you may grow into all He has for your life.

Wisdom is sweet to your soul.
If you find it, you will have a bright future,
and your hopes will not be cut short.

PROVERBS 24:14 NLT

You're worthy of the wonderful.
Believe it to receive it.

Marshawn Evans Daniels

Today I pray for an awakening! As you exit the old, I pray your next-level calling would rise up as God aligns you with your **warrior princess identity.**

He who was seated on the throne said,
"I am making everything new!"
Then He said, "Write this down, for
these words are trustworthy and true."
REVELATION 21:5 NIV

God loves us too much to leave us or lose us, so instead He shifts us so that true significance can flow from within us.

Marshawn Evans Daniels

God has chosen you to create the incredible. I'm praying you can accept the gift and grace of His favor, for His glory.

Good morning!
You're beautiful with God's beauty,
Beautiful inside and out!
God be with you.

LUKE 1:28 THE MESSAGE

Though we often struggle to believe we're divinely beautiful, beautiful is exactly who and what we are.

Marshawn Evans Daniels

DaySpring

God is taking you into new, bold adventures. You are chosen and ready. I'm praying that you'd not waste time questioning your worth and capacity, and instead enter this journey with joyous focus.

God deliberately chose men and women that the culture overlooks and exploits and abuses, chose these "nobodies" to expose the hollow pretensions of the "somebodies."
I CORINTHIANS 1:27 THE MESSAGE

An unashamed woman is an unstoppable woman.

Marshawn Evans Daniels

DaySpring

The Lord's significance defines your own. Your life is a bright and necessary light. I'm praying you embrace it today: you are enough, capable, and beyond worthy.

The lives of good people are brightly lit streets.

PROVERBS 13:9 THE MESSAGE

Someone is waiting on you to come out of hiding.
You matter more than you could ever imagine.

Marshawn Evans Daniels

DaySpring

I'm thanking God for the wisdom He gives. As you release what no longer belongs, including old ways, habits, and thoughts, I'm praying you'll live with a renewed sense of peace and serenity.

Do not conform to the pattern of this world, but be transformed by the renewing of your mind.

ROMANS 12:2 NIV

The mind of God is a majestic place to live.

Marshawn Evans Daniels

God has given you everything you need to fulfill your mission in this season. I'm praying that the Lord gives you courage to distinguish what you can do from what you are called to do.

To everyone who has will more be given, and he will have an abundance. But from the one who has not, even what he has will be taken away.

MATTHEW 25:29 ESV

It takes courage to say no to opportunity so that you can say yes to destiny.

Marshawn Evans Daniels

God has given you **intentional gifts** and **magnificent abilities.** I am praying that He would enlarge your territory, increase your wisdom, and bless everything your hands touch.

Each person is given something to do that shows who God is.
I CORINTHIANS 12:7 THE MESSAGE

God is growing your gifts for His glory.

Marshawn Evans Daniels

DaySpring

Your life is a supernatural bridge that connects others to bigger blessings. I'm asking God to show you where you can have a meaningful impact today.

If the willingness is there, the gift is acceptable according to what one has, not according to what one does not have.

II CORINTHIANS 8:12 NIV

You're right where you're supposed to be for God's next big move.

Marshawn Evans Daniels

God has made you a light that drives out the darkness. I'm praying that you dare to believe in your radiance, relevance, and readiness. Remember, nothing is impossible or too hard for the Lord!

He did not do many miracles there because of their lack of faith.
MATTHEW 13:58 NIV

Operate in your expectations, not your experiences.

Marshawn Evans Daniels

DaySpring

Now is the perfect time to go where God is guiding. May you trade perfectionism and procrastination for surrender and bold steps taken in expectant faith.

Do not despise these small beginnings, for the LORD rejoices to see the work begin.

ZECHARIAH 4:10 NLT

Starting before you're ready is the ultimate faith step, and faith steps are God's favorite kind of steps.

Marshawn Evans Daniels

You are made in God's image—and therefore more than enough! I'm asking Him to give you supernatural courage to live worthy and ready.

Fear of man is a dangerous trap,
but to trust in God means safety.
PROVERBS 29:25 TLB

When God sees you, He sees the piece
of Himself He placed in only you.

Marshawn Evans Daniels

Investing in yourself and your God-given vision is a worthy investment. May God order and bless every decision you make to develop your capacity to change the world.

Where your treasure is, there your heart will be also.

MATTHEW 6:21 NIV

Self-investment is at the core of Kingdom leadership. It is impossible to get a return on an investment you never make.

Marshawn Evans Daniels

DaySpring

Know that you're capable and called to complete your mission **for such a time as this.** I'm praying the Lord focuses you as He **molds you** into a master finisher who shows others how to complete their missions too.

So now finish doing it as well, so that your readiness in desiring it may be matched by your completing it out of what you have.

II CORINTHIANS 8:11 ESV

Finish what you've started. All of heaven rejoices when you cross the finish line.

Marshawn Evans Daniels

I asked God to guide you every step of the way as you fully and fearlessly take on the adventure ahead.
Step in. You're ready.

You have not passed this way before.

JOSHUA 3:4 ESV

You're a masterpiece—and an essential component in God's master plan.

Marshawn Evans Daniels